D0911373

PRAYING
GOD'S
WORD

PRAYING GOD'S WORD

ED DUFRESNE

Whitaker House

PRAYING GOD'S WORD

ISBN: 0-88368-240-0
Printed in the United States of America
Copyright © 1982 by Ed Dufresne

Whitaker House
30 Hunt Valley Circle
New Kensington, PA 15068

No part of this book may be reproduced or transmitted in any
form or by any means, electronic or mechanical, including
photocopying, recording, or by any information storage and
retrieval system, without permission in writing from the
publisher.

4 5 6 7 8 9 10 11 12 13 14 / 06 05 04 03 02 01 00 99 98 97

Contents

Preface

This book has been written by the Holy Spirit, because it is all the Word of God. I believe in giving honor where it is due by thanking Kathy Palmer, Cathy Wendell, and the staff at Ed Dufresne Ministries for all their hard work and time spent in putting this book together.

The purpose of this book is to help you develop an accurate prayer life that's based on God's Word and to help you grow spiritually and benefit the Body of Christ. Now get ready to enter into an exciting time of prayer.

—Ed Dufresne

Introduction

Under the New Covenant in which we are living, God has given us a new life and a new way we believers are to live.

First of all He tells us, *For therein is the righteousness of God revealed from faith to faith: as it is written, The just shall live by faith* (Rom. 1:17). So, faith is a way of life to the believer.

He also tells us, "Pray at all times—on every occasion, in every season—in the Spirit, with all [manner of] prayer and entreaty. To that end keep alert and watch with strong purpose and perseverance, interceding in behalf of all the saints (God's consecrated people)" (Eph. 6:18 AMP).

We can see from the preceding scriptures that faith and prayer are to be a way of life for us as believers.

In this book we will endeavor to help you develop a consistent and accurate prayer life. Only as the Church prays will she take her rightful place in the earth. Only as Christians pray will we see God move in the way we desire and, also, in the way He desires. With our prayers we will have to give birth in the spirit to the great moves and manifestations of God's Spirit in these last days.

Ephesians 6:18 in the *King James Version* says, *Praying always with all prayer and supplication in the Spirit.* God's Word tells us to pray with all manner of prayer. In the light of the above scripture, we will endeavor to cover all kinds of prayer in this book.

The prayer of intercession, or intercessory prayer, has been an almost lost art to the Church. But in this end time God is bringing it to the forefront and bringing much enlightenment on this subject. Intercession will cause God's will, which is His Word, to be established on the earth. So, along with praying God's Word we must apply the prayer of intercession to bring the will of God to pass on the earth.

Ephesians 6:12 says, *For we wrestle not against flesh and blood, but against principalities, against powers, against the rulers of the darkness of this world, against spiritual wickedness in high places.*

Second Corinthians 4:3,4 says, *But if our gospel be hid, it is hid to them that are lost: in whom the god of this world hath blinded the minds of them which believe not, lest the light of the glorious gospel of Christ, who is the image of God, should shine unto them.*

First John 5:19 says, *And we know that we are of God, and the whole world lieth in wickedness.*

The Scriptures call Satan *the god of this world.* He rules over nations, cities, towns; over people who are not born again. In the spirit realm just above the earth, Satan has built spiritual fortresses, strongholds from which he rules over nations, cities, and kingdoms of this world.

But, praise God, the good news for the Church is that he doesn't rule over us! Colossians 1:13 AMP states, ''The Father has delivered us and drawn us to Himself out of the control and the dominion of darkness and has transferred us into the kingdom of the Son of His love.''

Ephesians 2:6 AMP states, ''And He raised us up together with Him and made us sit down together—giving us joint seating with Him—in the heavenly sphere'' (that is, far above Satan's kingdom) ''[by virtue of our being] in Christ Jesus, the Messiah, the Anointed One.''

Now Jesus has given the Church His authority, His name, and His power. It is up to us to use that authority against

Satan. *Or else how can one enter into a strong man's house, and spoil his goods, except he first bind the strong man? and then he will spoil his house* (Matt. 12:29).

For though we walk in the flesh, we do not war after the flesh: (for the weapons of our warfare are not carnal, but mighty through God to the pulling down of strong holds) (2 Cor. 10:3,4).

The Word of God is talking about satanic strongholds. It is the responsibility of the Church to bind Satan up and cast him down so that the will of God, which is His Word, can be established in the earth.

Praying God's Word and interceding for the will of God to be established will cause changes in our communities, churches, and homes. This will cause changes not only in our nation, but in the other nations of the world as well.

To bring forth the manifestation of God's will on the earth, we're going to

13

have to battle with the spirit forces of evil in the realm of intercession, then speak God's creative Word over situations that need to be changed.

As we do this, the Spirit of God will have the liberty He needs to move in the earth. Then we will see the light of God begin to penetrate the areas of darkness.

In Jesus' name, our prayer is that the Holy Spirit will use this book as a tool for uniting the members of His Body with one another and with Him to bring faith and give birth to the greatest revival this world has ever seen.

The Staff of
Ed Dufresne Ministries

Abbreviations

AMP   *The Amplified Bible.*

ASV   *American Standard Version.*

Bar   *The New Testament: A New Translation. (William Barclay.)*

Knox   *The New Testament in the Translation of Monsignor Ronald Knox.*

Mof   *The Bible. A New Translation. (James Moffatt.)*

Phi   *The New Testament in Modern English. (J. B. Phillips.)*

TLB   *The Living Bible.*

TCNT   *The Twentieth Century New Testament.*

Wey, Harp	*Weymouth's New Testament in Modern Speech.* (Richard Francis Weymouth. Harper & Row, Publishers, Inc. and James Clarke and Company Ltd.)
Wey, Kreg	*New Testament In Modern Speech.* (Richard Francis Weymouth. Kregel Publications.)
Wuest	*The New Testament: An Expanded Translation.* (Kenneth S. Wuest.)

1
Prayers of
Praise and Worship

Spiritual Preparation for Prayer: Developing a Spirit of Prayer by Fellowshipping with the Father.

As believers it is extremely important that we develop good spiritual habits. We must learn to discipline ourselves and become diligent seekers of God.

The Word of God and the practice of prayer must be foremost in our lives and something that we look forward to and enjoy every day. Prayer should be the most enjoyable part of our day because it is the time that we visit with the Father, the Lord Jesus, and the Holy Spirit.

Just being in the presence of God changes us. There is peace and tranquility that surrounds and flows from us which even others can sense.

Every Christian should develop his own prayer life and daily set aside a certain time to visit with the Father. Doing this is a key to a victorious walk with God.

The early Church set a time apart for daily prayer. *Now Peter and John went up together into the temple at **the hour of prayer**, being the ninth hour* (Acts 3:1).

When we study the Gospels, we see that Jesus sometimes spent all night in prayer. *But we will give ourselves continually to prayer, and to the ministry of the word* (Acts 6:4).

As we attend to God's Word and prayer, more and more enlightenment will come on the subject. The Spirit of God has shown us some important things in the area of spiritual preparation for this kind of prayer life. These things have been a blessing to us. We believe that you will be able to apply them in your prayer life and that they will bless you, also.

We have found fellowshipping with and ministering to the Lord to be the most enjoyable and satisfying part of our lives. There is something about fellowshipping with God that seems to translate us right into His holy presence, right into what seems to be the very atmosphere of heaven.

This time spent in worship and praise is vital because it brings us into a new realm in Him. It causes us to be renewed and strengthened with His life and brings us to know Him more intimately.

Praising and worshiping our heavenly Father is something special, precious, and personal. It is between you and God. You share this time together. We were created for companionship with God, and He longs for each one of His children to set apart a time to get to know Him.

Developing an attitude of worship and praise and progressing toward continuous fellowship with God will cause you to be edified. You will grow in grace and be given to a spirit of prayer. You will be in a position to hear God.

The Holy Spirit will begin to use you when He needs someone to pray for an urgent matter. You will be available because you have taken the time to stir up the gift within. You have built yourself up on your most holy faith by praying in the Holy Ghost.

Being used in this ministry to the Lord is what you have been created for.

Meditate on the following scriptures. Personalize them, confess them, and let the Holy Spirit minister to you concerning them.

20

1 Corinthians 1:9

God is faithful, by whom ye were called unto the fellowship of his Son Jesus Christ our Lord.

Fellowship (Greek: *koinonia*) means "communion; fellowship; sharing in common; inner communing of spirits."

"God will surely do this for you, for he always does just what he says, and he is the one who invited you into this wonderful friendship with his Son, even Christ our Lord" (TLB).

"You can rely on God by whom you were called to share the life of his Son, Jesus Christ, our Lord" (Bar).

"God is faithful—reliable, trustworthy and [therefore] ever true to His promise, and He can be depended on; by Him you were called into companionship and participation with His Son, Jesus Christ our Lord" (AMP).

21

1 Corinthians 2:9-12

But as it is written, Eye hath not seen, nor ear heard, neither have entered into the heart of man, the things which God hath prepared for them that love him.

But God hath revealed them unto us by his Spirit: for the Spirit searcheth all things, yea, the deep things of God.

''Things which eye saw not, and ear heard not, and which entered not into the heart of man, whatsoever things God prepared for them that love him.

''Thus God has, through the Spirit, let us share his secret. For nothing is hidden from the Spirit, not even the deep wisdom of God.

''For who could really understand a man's inmost thoughts except the spirit of the man himself? How much less could anyone understand the thoughts of God except the very Spirit of God?

''We have now received not the spirit of the world but the Spirit of God himself, so that we can understand something of God's generosity towards us'' (Phi).

"That is what is meant by the Scriptures which say that no mere man has ever seen, heard or even imagined what wonderful things God has ready for those who love the Lord. But we know about these things because God has sent His Spirit to tell us, and His Spirit searches out and shows us all of God's deepest secrets'' (TLB).

As you begin to meditate on these scriptures, pray and worship God in the Spirit. Thank God for His wonderful call to fellowship and that His Spirit reveals the deep things of God to your spirit. Thus, becoming ever conscious of the presence of God, you develop an attitude of prayer.

Hebrews 13:15

By him therefore let us offer the sacrifice of praise to God continually, that is, the fruit of our lips giving thanks to his name.

"Through him, therefore, let us offer a constant sacrifice of praise to God—the tribute of lips which openly acknowledge his name" (Phi).

"Through Him therefore let us constantly and at all times offer up to God a sacrifice of praise, which is the fruit of lips that thankfully acknowledge and confess and glorify His name" (AMP).

Continue to have an attitude of praise. God inhabits praise, so the presence of God will begin to move upon us as we worship the Lord.

Minister to the Lord with the Psalms. Make up your own psalms as you go along. Sing to the Lord or just speak them to Him.

Paul says, *I will pray with the spirit, and I will pray with the understanding also: I will sing with the spirit, and I will sing with the understanding also* (1 Cor. 14:15).

As you worship and praise God in the Spirit and find portions of Scripture that talk about His attributes, His Person, speak those out of your heart. Use the scriptures in this book and find your own.

As you worship God, your scope of Him widens. God becomes greater to you; God inhabits the praises of His people. Even as you do this, you bring His Presence on the scene.

Colossians 3:16

''Let the teaching concerning Christ remain as a rich treasure in your hearts. In all wisdom teach and admonish one another with psalms, hymns, and spiritual songs, and sing with grace in your hearts to God'' (Wey, Kreg).

Let the word of Christ dwell in you richly in all wisdom; teaching and admonishing one another in psalms and hymns and spiritual songs, singing with grace in your hearts to the Lord.

Psalm 3:3-6

But thou, O Lord, art a shield for me; my glory, and the lifter up of mine head.

I cried unto the Lord with my voice, and he heard me out of his holy hill. I laid me down and slept; I awaked; for the Lord sustained me.

I will not be afraid of ten thousands of people, that have set themselves against me round about.

Psalm 5:1-3,7,11,12

Give ear to my words, O Lord, consider my meditation. Hearken unto the voice of my cry, my king, and my God: for unto thee will I pray. My voice shalt thou hear in the morning, O Lord; in the morning will I direct my prayer unto thee, and will look up.

But as for me, I will come into thy house in the multitude of thy mercy: and in thy fear will I worship toward thy holy temple.

But let all those that put their trust in thee rejoice: let them ever shout for joy, because thou defendest them: let them also that love thy name be joyful in thee. For thou, Lord, wilt bless the righteous; with favour wilt thou compass him as with a shield.

Psalm 8:1,2,9

O Lord our Lord, how excellent is thy name in all the earth! who hast set thy glory above the heavens.

Out of the mouth of babes and sucklings hast thou ordained strength because of thine enemies, that thou mightest still the enemy and the avenger.

O Lord our Lord, how excellent is thy name in all the earth!

Psalm 9:1,2

I will praise thee, O Lord, with my whole heart; I will shew forth all thy marvellous works. I will be glad and rejoice in thee: I will sing praise to thy name, O thou most High.

Psalm 16:11

Thou wilt shew me the path of life: in thy presence is fulness of joy; at thy right hand there are pleasures for evermore.

Psalm 17:15

As for me, I will behold thy face in righteousness: I shall be satisfied, when I awake, with thy likeness.

Psalm 18:46

The Lord liveth; and blessed be my rock; and let the God of my salvation be exalted.

Psalm 19:14

Let the words of my mouth, and the meditation of my heart, be acceptable in thy sight, O Lord, my strength, and my redeemer.

Psalm 20:5–7

We will rejoice in thy salvation, and in the name of our God we will set up our banners: the Lord fulfil all thy petitions.

Now know I that the Lord saveth his anointed; he will hear him from his holy heaven with the saving strength of his right hand.

Some trust in chariots, and some in horses: but we will remember the name of the Lord our God.

Psalm 21:13

Be thou exalted, Lord, in thine own strength: so will we sing and praise thy power.

Psalm 22:3

But thou art holy, O thou that inhabitest the praises of Israel.

Psalm 24:3-6

Who shall ascend into the hill of the Lord? or who shall stand in his holy place? He that hath clean hands, and a pure heart; who hath not lifted up his soul unto vanity, nor sworn deceitfully.

He shall receive the blessing from the Lord, and righteousness from the God of his salvation. This is the generation of them that seek him, that seek thy face, O Jacob.

Psalm 25:1,4-6

Unto thee, O Lord, do I lift up my soul.

Shew me thy ways, O Lord; teach me thy paths. Lead me in thy truth, and teach me: for thou art the God of my salvation; on thee do I wait all the day.

Remember, O Lord, thy tender mercies and thy lovingkindnesses; for they have been ever of old.

Psalm 27:14

Wait on the Lord: be of good courage, and he shall strengthen thine heart: wait, I say, on the Lord.

Psalm 34:1-4

I will bless the Lord at all times: his praise shall continually be in my mouth. My soul shall make her boast in the Lord: the humble shall hear thereof, and be glad.

O magnify the Lord with me, and let us exalt his name together. I sought the Lord, and he heard me, and delivered me from all my fears.

Psalm 35:27,28

Let them shout for joy, and be glad, that favour my righteous cause: yea, let them say continually, Let the Lord be magnified, which hath pleasure in the prosperity of his servant. And my tongue shall speak of thy righteousness and of thy praise all the day long.

Psalm 36:8-10

They shall be abundantly satisfied with the fatness of thy house; and thou shalt make them drink of the river of thy pleasures. For with thee is the fountain of life: in thy light shall we see light.

O continue thy lovingkindness unto them that know thee; and thy righteousness to the upright in heart.

Psalm 46:10,11

Be still, and know that I am God: I will be exalted among the heathen, I will be exalted in the earth. The Lord of hosts is with us; the God of Jacob is our refuge.

Psalm 48:1

Great is the Lord, and greatly to be praised in the city of our God, in the mountain of his holiness.

Psalm 49:3

My mouth shall speak of wisdom; and the meditation of my heart shall be of understanding.

Psalm 63:2-6

. . . To see thy power and thy glory, so as I have seen thee in the sanctuary.

Because thy lovingkindness is better than life, my lips shall praise thee. Thus will I bless thee while I live: I will lift up my hands in thy name.

My soul shall be satisfied as with marrow and fatness; and my mouth shall praise thee with joyful lips: when I remember thee upon my bed, and meditate on thee in the night watches.

Psalm 65:1-4

Praise waiteth for thee, O God, in Sion: and unto thee shall the vow be performed.

O thou that hearest prayer, unto thee shall all flesh come. Iniquities prevail against me: as for our transgressions, thou shalt purge them away.

Blessed is the man whom thou choosest, and causest to approach unto thee, that he may dwell in the courts: we shall be satisfied with the goodness of thy house, even of thy holy temple.

Psalm 84

How amiable are thy tabernacles, O Lord of hosts! My soul longeth, yea, even fainteth for the courts of the Lord: my heart and my flesh crieth out for the living God.

Yea, the sparrow hath found an house, and the swallow a nest for herself, where she may lay her young, even thine altars, O Lord of hosts, my King, and my God.

Blessed are they that dwell in thy house: they will be still praising thee. Blessed is the man whose strength is in thee; in whose heart are the ways of them. Who passing through the valley of Baca make it a well; the rain also filleth the pools. They go from strength to strength, every one of them in Zion appeareth before God.

O Lord God of hosts, hear my prayer: give ear, O God of Jacob. Behold, O God our shield, and look upon the face of thine anointed. For a day in thy courts is better than a thousand. I had rather be a door-keeper in the house of my God, than to dwell in the tents of wickedness.

For the Lord God is a sun and shield: the Lord will give grace and glory: no good thing will he withhold from them that walk uprightly.

O Lord of hosts, blessed is the man that trusteth in thee.

Psalm 89:15-18

Blessed is the people that know the joyful sound: they shall walk, O Lord, in the light of thy countenance. In thy name shall they rejoice all the day: and in thy righteousness shall they be exalted.

For thou art the glory of their strength: and in thy favour our horn shall be exalted. For the Lord is our defence; and the Holy One of Israel is our king.

Psalm 91:1,2

He that dwelleth in the secret place of the most High shall abide under the shadow of the Almighty. I will say of the Lord, He is my refuge and my fortress: my God; in him will I trust.

Psalm 93:1

The Lord reigneth, he is clothed with majesty; the Lord is clothed with strength, wherewith he hath girded himself: the world also is stablished, that it cannot be moved.

Psalm 104:1,2

Bless the Lord, O my soul. O Lord my God, thou art very great; thou art clothed with honour and majesty. Who coverest thyself with light as with a garment: who stretchest out the heavens like a curtain.

Psalm 107:1,2

O give thanks unto the Lord, for he is good: for his mercy endureth for ever.

Let the redeemed of the Lord say so, whom he hath redeemed from the hand of the enemy.

2
Intercession—
What It Is

First of all, let's lay the foundation by understanding what intercession is.

Intercessory prayer is standing in the gap or taking the place of another. Primarily, it is done in the spirit. But in some instances, particularly when you know what God's will is, you pray in the understanding. This section of the book will deal with intercession done in the Spirit.

The greatest thing you will ever learn about intercessory prayer, the greatest help, is to depend on the Holy Spirit. This is the key: learning to understand the Spirit of God, learning to depend on Him for your prayer life.

The Holy Spirit is God. You can praise Him, learn to communicate with Him, and *trust* and acknowledge His presence in you. He is a Person. He lives in you and has been sent to help you.

John 14:26

''But the Comforter (Counselor, Helper, Intercessor, Advocate, Strengthener, Standby), the Holy Spirit, Whom the Father will send in My name [in My place, to represent Me and act on My behalf], He will teach you all things. And He will cause you to recall—will remind you of, bring to your remembrance—everything I have told you'' (AMP).

Learn to rely on the Holy Spirit's help as you pray.

John 16:13

"But when He, the Spirit of Truth (the truth-giving Spirit) comes, He will guide you into all the truth—the whole, full truth. For He will not speak His own message—on His own authority—but He will tell whatever He hears [from the Father, He will give the message that has been given to Him] and He will announce and declare to you the things that are to come—that will happen in the future" (AMP).

If you have been filled with the Holy Spirit, then He is in you to do these things. Learn to yield yourself to Him as you pray in tongues.

John 7:37,38

"Now on the final and most important day of the feast, Jesus stood forth and He cried in a loud voice, If any man is thirsty, let him come to Me and drink!

41

''He who believes in Me—who cleaves to and trusts in and relies on Me—as the Scripture has said, Out from his innermost being springs and rivers of living water shall flow (continuously)'' (AMP).

The Holy Spirit lives in you to be a Helper and to bring a continuous flow of the Life of God. That river flows through every believer. When you yield to that life and love in your prayer life, it will bring the power of God into the human race and set them free. Giving the Spirit of God the right of way will cause a whole new dimension to open up for you in prayer.

As you yield to the Holy Spirit and flow in the compassion of God, great results will follow. It's the love of God or the God-kind of love—**Agape**—flowing through you for this world, for your brothers and sisters, for those who are sick, that will bring their deliverance.

Love is the most powerful ingredient to your intercession, because God is love (John 4:8) *and love never fails* (1 Cor. 13:8). Romans 5:5 states, *The love of God is shed abroad in our hearts by the Holy Ghost which is given unto us.*

John 3:16

For God so loved the world, that he gave his only begotten Son, that whosoever believeth in him should not perish, but have everlasting life.

1 John 3:16

Hereby perceive we the love of God, because he laid down his life for us: and we ought to lay down our lives for the brethren.

This means to take a time when you set your needs and interests aside and take upon yourself the needs of others in prayer. This is the God-kind of love in action. When it is applied with the prayer of intercession, it is powerful! Your time in worship and praise will bring you to that place of compassion which will allow the Holy Spirit to flow through you.

WHERE TO BEGIN IN INTERCESSION
1 Timothy 2:1-5

I exhort therefore, that, first of all, supplications, prayers, intercessions, and giving of thanks, be made for all men; for kings, and for all that are in authority; that we may lead a quiet and peaceable life in all godliness and honesty.

For this is good and acceptable in the sight of God our Saviour; Who will have all men to be saved, and to come unto the knowledge of the truth. For there is one God, and one mediator between God and men, the man Christ Jesus.

Ephesians 6:18,19

Praying always with all prayer and supplication in the Spirit, and watching thereunto with all perseverance and

supplication for all saints; and for me, that
utterance may be given unto me, that I may
open my mouth boldly, to make known the
mystery of the gospel.

The above scriptures give us some
guidelines to use in our intercession.
Intercession is to be made in the order
listed below. Intercede for:

1. all men.
2. kings (leaders of nations).
3. all in authority.
4. a quiet and peaceable life.
5. all saints.
6. gift ministries such as: apostles/
   missionaries, prophets, evangelists, pastors, and teachers.
7. divine utterance to be given to
   those who minister so that they
   are able to minister with freedom
   the mystery of Christ.

As you flow in the compassion of
God for all men (mentioned above), let
the Holy Spirit make the intercession
through you. Then the love of God for

them will flow through your being. Just yield to it.

As you continue on in your prayer time, there might come a desire within your spirit to groan or bear down as if you were going to have a baby. Yield to it. That is the Holy Spirit using you to give birth to babies being born into the Kingdom.

Isaiah 66:8

Who hath heard such a thing? who hath seen such things? Shall the earth be made to bring forth in one day? or shall a nation be born at once? for as soon as Zion travailed, she brought forth her children.

There is something very important that we must learn: This kind of praying is a key to the great revival of these last days. All the great moves and manifestations of the Spirit of God must be borne in the Spirit by groanings and travail. We must bring them forth from the ''bowels'' of our being. The Church (Zion) must begin to give birth now!

Unless someone intercedes, there are those who will never be saved—the Devil has too great a hold on them. Unless someone stands in the gap, there are some who will never be healed. We need people who are willing to be intercessors.

Intercession must be made for all nations, for people everywhere. It will tear down the Devil's strongholds and cause God's will to be established on earth. It will bring the outpouring of God's Spirit.

Let us now study different translations of the same scriptures to bring more light into the subject of intercession.

James 5:16

The effectual fervent prayer of a righteous man availeth much.

"The supplication of a righteous man availeth much in its working" (ASV).

47

"Powerful is the heartfelt supplication of a righteous man" (Wey, Harp).

"The prayers of the righteous have a powerful effect" (Mof).

"Tremendous power is made available through a good man's earnest prayer" (Phi).

"Great is the power of a good man's fervent prayer" (TCNT).

"When a just man prays fervently there is great virtue in his prayer" (Knox).

"The heartfelt supplication of a righteous man exerts a mighty influence" (Wey, Kreg).

"The earnest (heartfelt, continued) prayer of a righteous man makes tremendous power available—dynamic in its working" (AMP).

Heartfelt means "deeply felt, earnest, sincere."

Avail means "to be of use, advantage, or profit; to prevail against (said of spiritual enemies)."

Power (Greek: *dunamis*) means "ability, might."

Romans 8:26,27

Likewise the Spirit also helpeth our infirmities: for we know not what we should pray for as we ought: but the Spirit itself maketh intercession for us with groanings which cannot be uttered.

And he that searcheth the hearts knoweth what is the mind of the Spirit, because he maketh intercession for the saints according to the will of God.

"In the same way the Spirit also helps us in our weakness; for we do not know what prayers to offer nor in what way to offer them.

"But the Spirit Himself pleads for us in yearnings that can find no words, and the Searcher of hearts knows what the Spirit's meaning is, because His intercessions for God's people are in harmony with God's will" (Wey, Kreg).

"Even so, the Spirit helps us in our weaknesses. We do not know what to pray for, if we are to pray as we ought, but the Spirit himself intercedes for us, when the only prayers that we can offer are inarticulate cries.

"He who penetrates into the inmost depths of the human heart knows what the Spirit means, for it is by God's will that the Spirit pleads for God's people" (Bar).

Certainly, situations arise when we do have a knowledge of how to pray in our own understanding. And we should. Many times, however, we have no idea of how to pray.

For instance, we could not possibly know in our understanding when a missionary somewhere across the world is in trouble. But the Holy Spirit knows all things. Through you, as you make yourself available in intercession, He will get God's will for that missionary.

Because we have an understanding of how God's Word says to pray for our nation, we should pray for it with the understanding. However, many things happen that we have no knowledge of in our understanding.

The Holy Spirit knows God's will. As you intercede, the Holy Spirit will help you. In the spirit you will tear down Satan's strongholds, stop his plan against our nation, and defeat all his other purposes.

1 Corinthians 14:15

What is it then? I will pray with the spirit, and I will pray with the understanding also: I will sing with the spirit, and I will sing with the understanding also.

2 Corinthians 10:3,4

For though we walk in the flesh, we do not war after the flesh: (For the weapons of our warfare are not carnal, but mighty through God to the pulling down of strong holds).

Ephesians 6:12-18

For we wrestle not against flesh and blood, but against principalities, against powers, against the rulers of the darkness of this world, against spiritual wickedness in high places.

Wherefore take unto you the whole armour of God, that ye may be able to withstand in the evil day, and having done all, to stand.

Stand therefore, having your loins girt about with truth, and having on the breastplate of righteousness; and your feet shod with the preparation of the gospel of peace; above all, taking the shield of faith, wherewith ye shall be able to quench all the fiery darts of the wicked.

And take the helmet of salvation, and the sword of the Spirit, which is the word of God: praying always with all prayer and supplication in the Spirit, and watching thereunto with all perseverance and supplication for all saints.

The warfare that this scripture talks about takes place in the spirit. The Holy Spirit will help you in intercession.

Intercession must take place in order for people to be born again. As we saw in Isaiah 66:8, Zion is the Church. So, the Church must travail in intercession for babies to be born. Intercession and travail will bring the people for whom we are praying to a position of being ready to receive Christ. It will cause a spirit of repentance to come on them. In order for us to see great moves of God's Spirit and thousands of people born again into the Kingdom of God, there must be intercession.

Intercession must be made a second time for the new Christian. We all know Christians who seem to stumble and fall, never seeming to grow properly in the things of God. We need to intercede so that Christ may be properly formed in them.

Galatians 4:19

My little children, of whom I travail in birth again until Christ be formed in you....

"Striving with intense effort and anguish until Christ be outwardly expressed in you" (Wuest).

"My dear children—you for whom I am again enduring mother's pains, till a likeness of Christ shall have been formed in you" (TCNT).

"Oh, my dear children, I feel the pangs of childbirth all over again till Christ be formed within you, and how I long to be with you now!" (Phi).

Ministers Need Our Prayers, Too

As believers, it is our responsibility to pray for the members of the Body of

Christ whom God has placed in authority. Praying for ministers gives us a part in the job God called them to do. We help to bring forth their ministries.

Ephesians 6:19

And for me (Paul), *that utterance may be given unto me, that I may open my mouth boldly, to make known the mystery of the gospel.*

2 Corinthians 1:11

Ye also helping together by prayer for us, that for the gift bestowed upon us by the means of many persons thanks may be given by many on our behalf.

The above scripture is very descriptive of prayer for ministries. Paul tells the Corinthians that their prayers for him, for the gift that God bestowed upon him, will cause many people to give thanks to God.

The Corinthians were helping Paul's effectiveness in his ministry through

their prayers, which resulted in the
salvation of many. So it is today as we
pray for the fivefold ministries—
apostles, prophets, evangelists, pastors,
and teachers—to go forth in full power.
In helping them by our prayers, we
function as one united Body in the
earth.

3
Praying God's Word

Prayer for
the Body of Christ

The Bible says in James 3:16, *For where envying and strife is, there is confusion and every evil work.*

One of the biggest problems the Body of Christ has had is fussing and fighting with one another. This has not been a good testimony to the world and has stopped the flow of God's power in the lives of those who are in strife with one another.

Use the following confession to pray for your local body of believers and the Body of Christ everywhere. God has

57

moved miraculously among church groups as people have confessed God's Word over situations instead of talking about problems and each other.

As you pray this prayer, we believe that you will be set free from frustration and worry about your brothers and sisters in the Lord. You will witness a change in Christians all over the world.

Remember, there is no distance in the spirit world. You can pray this prayer wherever you are. God will use *your* faith to get what it says done—even across the world!

Father, in Jesus' name, I bring before You the body of believers of _____ and of the rest of the world.

Through faith in Your Word, I confess with my mouth that we never let any foul or polluting language, evil word, or unwholesome and worthless talk come out our mouths. We speak only what is good and beneficial to the spiritual progress of others. The words we speak fit the need and occasion, so that they are a blessing and give grace to those who hear.

I say that we have banished from us all bitterness, indignation, and wrath (passion, rage, bad temper); resentment (anger, animosity); quarreling (brawling, clamor, contention); slander (evil speaking, abusive or blasphemous language); and malice (spite, ill will, or baseness of any kind).

We have become useful, helpful, tenderhearted (compassionate, understanding, loving hearted), and kind to one another. We have readily and freely forgiven one another as You, in Christ, forgave us.

Thank You, Father, that we walk in love—esteeming and delighting in one another—as Christ loved us and, as a slain offering and sacrifice to You, gave Himself up for us.

I say, in Jesus' name, that we continue in prayer and watch, with thanksgiving, that our prayers avail much, because we have been made righteous through Jesus. I thank You that You watch over Your Word to perform it.

I believe that I have received this according to Mark 11:23,24, in Jesus' name. Amen.

Scripture References

Eph. 4:29,31,32 AMP	James 5:16
Eph. 5:1,2 AMP	1 Cor. 1:30
Col. 4:2	

Praying God's Word

Additional Scriptures

Mark 16:17,18,20	Eph. 5:17-19
John 14:27	Eph. 6:10-19
Acts 22:14	Phil. 1:9-11
Rom. 8:4,5	Col. 1:9-14
1 Cor. 13:4-8	2 Thess. 3:11,12
Eph. 4:23,24	Heb. 13:20,21

Prayer for Ministries and Ministers

For Ministries

Following is a list of scriptures to pray for ministries. By no means is it complete, but it will serve as a good foundation. Be alert in finding other scriptures to pray, especially from the book of Acts. Name those you want, but always include every person throughout the whole earth who is responsible for spreading the Good News.

For those ministries in error in certain areas, use scriptures about God revealing the truth to them. (See Eph. 1:17,18 and Job 22:30 AMP.)

Remember, God is no respecter of persons, so expect results!

Deuteronomy 28:1-14

Confess in the name of Jesus:

Every person involved in this ministry listens diligently to the voice of the Lord their

God, being watchful to do all His commandments.

All the blessings of verses 3-13 have come upon this ministry and overtaken it because everyone involved heeds the voice of the Lord . . . (Continue confessing the Scripture verses.)

Joshua 1:5-9

Confess that no person or persons shall be able to stand before those in positions of authority in this ministry all the days of their lives. As God was with Moses, so He will be with them. He will not fail nor forsake them.

Confess that they are strong (confident) and of good courage. Confess that they shall cause people to inherit the land (promises) which God swore to their fathers to give them . . . (Continue confessing the Scripture verses.)

1 Samuel 3:19,20

Confess that the Lord is with the prophets who are involved in this ministry and that He lets none of their words fall to the ground. Confess that people all over the earth know they are established to be prophets of the Lord.

Psalm 1:1-3

Confess that the people involved in this ministry are blessed, happy, fortunate, prosperous, and enviable, because they walk and live not in the counsel of the ungodly (following their advice, their plans, and their purposes).

They do not stand (submissive and inactive) in the path where sinners walk, nor do they sit down where the scornful (and mockers) gather. Their delight and desire is in the law of the Lord . . . (Continue confessing the Scripture verses.)

Psalm 19:14

Confess that the words of their mouths and the meditation of their hearts are acceptable in God's sight . . . (continue).

Psalm 31:18-20

Confess that the lying lips, which speak against them, have been silenced . . .

Isaiah 58:6-14

Confess that they live a fasted life and that they have chosen God's fast. Confess that the bonds of wickedness are loosed . . .

Malachi 3:8-12

Pray for the people who make up local churches and those who support the ministries. Confess that they do not rob nor defraud God, that they do not withhold their tithes and offerings, that they are not cursed with the curse . . .

John 15:15,16

Confess that Jesus no longer calls those involved in this ministry servants . . .

Acts 1:8,14; 2:4,41-43,46,47; 3:6-9; 4:13,29,30,33; 5:12,14-16,38,39

Confess that the doctrines of this ministry are not of human origin and that it will not fail, be overthrown, or come to nothing. Because it is of God, no one will be able to stop, overthrow, or destroy it. Anyone trying to do so will be found fighting against God . . .

Acts 5:42

Confess that in spite of threats they never cease for a single day to teach . . .

Acts 6:4,7,8,10; 7:10; 8:6-8; 11:21-24

Confess that they have favor in the sight of all people.

Additional Scriptures

Ps. 91	Phil. 1:9-11
Prov. 2:10-16	Col. 1:9-14
4:8	3:16,17
Is. 54:14,15,17	4:2-6
Mark 16:15,17,18,20	2 Thess. 1:11,12
Luke 6:38	3:2,3
1 Cor. 13:4-8	1 Tim. 4:12-16
2 Cor. 9:8-11	2 Tim. 3:16,17
Eph. 3:16-19	Heb. 4:12
4:14,15,29-32	1 John 2:20,27
5:1-4,6-11	

For Ministers

Here is a prayer directly from the Bible that you may pray for ministers. It will bring results in the lives of ministers, Sunday school or Bible teachers, or anyone responsible for publishing the Gospel in any way.

As you pray it, mention the names of those for whom you are specifically praying; then include every person throughout the whole earth who is sharing the Gospel in any way.

Father, in Jesus' name, I confess that the men and women responsible for giving out

Your Gospel have been given the spirit of
wisdom and revelation in the knowledge of
You. Because the eyes of their understanding
have been enlightened, they know what is the
hope of Your calling and what the riches of the
glory of Your inheritance are in them. They
know what the exceeding greatness of Your
power is to them who believe.

I thank You, Father, that they continue in
prayer, watching with thanksgiving. I thank
You that You are opening unto them doors of
utterance to speak the mystery of Christ,
making that mystery manifest as they ought to
speak.

I thank You that they walk in wisdom
toward those who are without, redeeming the
time. I confess that they know how they ought
to answer every man.

Because of faith in Your Word, I say with my
mouth that they are filled with the knowledge
of Your will in all wisdom and spiritual
understanding. I say that they walk worthy of
You, Lord, unto all pleasing, being fruitful in
every good work and increasing in the
knowledge of You. Father, they are
strengthened with all might according to Your
glorious power, unto all patience and
longsuffering with joyfulness.

I give thanks unto You, Father, for making them partakers of the inheritance of the saints in light, for delivering them from the power of darkness, and for translating them into the Kingdom of Your dear Son. I confess that, speaking the truth in love, they are growing up into Him in all things, which is the Head, even Christ.

Father, Your Word which they speak is quick, powerful, and sharper than any two-edged sword, piercing even to the dividing asunder of soul and spirit, and of the joints and marrow. It is a discerner of the thoughts and intents of the heart.

They have an unction from the Holy One and know all things. The anointing which they have received of You abides in them; they need not that any man teach them. As the same anointing teaches them of all things and is truth and is no lie—even as it has taught them—they shall abide in You.

I say that the lying lips, which speak grievous things proudly and contemptuously against these righteous men and women, are being put to silence.

Oh, how great is Your goodness which You have laid up for them that fear You, which You have wrought for them that trust in You before the sons of men! You shall hide them in the secret of Your presence from the pride of man. You shall keep them secretly in a pavilion from the strife of tongues. No weapon that is formed against them shall prosper. Every tongue that shall rise against them in judgment they shall condemn.

This is the heritage of the servants of the Lord, and their righteousness is of You. I thank You, Father, that You are watching over Your Word to perform these things in their lives. Amen.

Scripture References

Col. 1:9-13	Ps. 31:18-20
Eph. 4:15	Is. 54:17
Heb. 4:12	Eph. 1:18,19
1 John 2:20,27	

Additional Scriptures

Is. 54:13-15	Mark 16:17,18,20

For Growth in Attendance

It is not God's will for churches and ministers to hold meetings which few people attend. Chapter 3 of the book of Acts reveals God's will: Thousands of people were added daily to the Church.

Pray the following confession from the Word for churches and ministries all over the world. **The Word works!** Remember what Jesus said in Mark 11:23, ''We will have what we say!''

Father, in Jesus' name, I bring before You (name the church or ministry for which you are praying). I say that the people involved in this ministry speak boldly, unfolding and proclaiming fully the mystery of Christ. They make it clear, as is their duty.

They constantly give praise to You. They have favor and goodwill with all the people, and You keep adding to their number daily those who are being saved from spiritual death.

Crowds of men and women who already acknowledge Jesus as their Savior and devote themselves to Him join those being added to Your Kingdom. The people gather also from the towns and hamlets round about the areas where the meetings are held. They bring other people who are sick or troubled with foul spirits, and all are cured.

As Your message keeps on spreading, Father, the number of disciples in these ministries continues to multiply greatly. The people are not able to resist the intelligence, wisdom, and inspiration of the Spirit with which Your ministers speak. With one accord great crowds of people listen to and heed what is said by (name of minister) as they hear and see the miracles and wonders which You keep performing. Foul spirits come out of many who are possessed by them. Many who are crippled or suffering from palsy are restored to health.

In the cities where the meetings are held, there is great rejoicing. Your presence is there with power, so that a great number of people learn to believe, adhere to, trust in, and rely on You. They learn to turn and surrender themselves to You, in Jesus' name.

Thank You, Father, for the privilege of praying. I expect results because Your Word does not return unto You void. Amen.

Now prepare for success; God cannot fail!

Scripture References (AMP)

Col. 4:4	Acts 8:6-8
Acts 2:47	11:21
5:14,16	Is. 55:11
6:7,10	

Prayer for Families

For Husbands
(to be prayed by wives)

Father, in Jesus' name, I pray and believe that _____ walks and lives not in the counsel of the ungodly, following their advice, plans, and purposes. He does not stand submissive and inactive in the path where sinners walk or sit down to relax and rest where the scornful and the mockers gather.

_____'s delight and desire is in Your Word. On Your precepts, instructions, and teachings he habitually meditates (ponders and studies) by day and by night.

Because he puts Your Word first place in his life, he is like a tree firmly planted and tended by the streams of water, ready to bring forth his fruit in its season. His leaf also does not fade or wither. Everything he does, including our life together, prospers and comes to maturity.

I thank You, Father, that _____ loves me; he is affectionate and sympathetic with me. I believe in Jesus' name that he is not harsh, bitter, or resentful toward me because he loves me, in a sense, as his own body.

I praise You that our fountain of human life is blessed with the rewards of fidelity, and he rejoices with me. I am as the loving hind and pleasant doe (tender, gentle, attractive). My bosom satisfies _____ at all times, and he is always transported with delight in my love. I rejoice, Father, that because Your Word is working in our marriage, _____ will never be infatuated with a loose woman, embrace the bosom of an outsider, or go astray. So be it!

Scripture References (AMP)

Ps. 1:1-3	Eph. 5:28
Col. 3:18,19	Prov. 5:15-20

If your husband is involved with another woman, pray Proverbs 2:16. Pray that discretion watches over him and understanding keeps him to deliver him from the alien woman, the outsider with her flattering words.

For Wives
(to be prayed by husbands)

Father, in Jesus' name, I pray and believe that _____ is a capable, intelligent, and virtuous woman. I praise You that I have found her. She is far more precious than jewels, and her value is far above rubies or pearls.

My heart trusts in her confidently and relies on and believes in her safely, so that I have no lack of honest gain or need of dishonest spoil. She will comfort, encourage, and do me only good as long as there is life within her.

Rising while yet it is night, she gets spiritual food for our household and assigns her maids their tasks. _____ expands prudently, not courting neglect of her present duties by assuming others.

She opens her mouth with skillful and godly wisdom. In her tongue is the law of kindness, giving counsel and instruction. _____ looks well to how things go in our household. The bread of idleness (gossip, discontent, and self-pity) she will not eat.

Father, I thank You that _____ respects and reverences me. She notices, regards, honors, prefers, venerates, and esteems me. She defers to me, praises me, loves and admires me exceedingly.

I praise You that Your Word is working in our marriage and that we have been transformed into the image of Jesus by the renewing of our minds. Amen.

Scripture References (AMP)
Prov. 31:10-12,15,16,26,27   Eph. 5:33

Additional Scriptures

Song of Sol. 1:2	1 Cor. 13:4-8
4:7,10	Eph. 4:15,29-32
5:16	5:1,2
7:10	Phil. 1:27
8:7	Col. 2:2
Matt. 19:6	4:6
Rom. 13:13	Titus 2:3-5
15:5-7	1 Pet. 3:1-9

For Children

Pray the following confession of faith (prayer), inserting the names of your children. We believe that when you do, you will be set free from worry and fear for them. God's Word will bring to pass the things that you desire for your children.

Father, in Jesus' name, I confess with my mouth, through faith in Your Word, that my children (name them) are taught of the Lord. Great is their peace.

I thank You that my children obey us, their parents, for it is right that they honor their father and mother. I thank You that, as You have promised, it is well with my children and that they will live long on the earth.

I confess that we, their parents, do not provoke them to wrath, but bring them up in the nurture and admonition of the Lord. Our children will not be discouraged.

We teach Your Word diligently unto our children. We talk of it when we sit in our house or walk by the way, when we lie down or rise up. We chasten our children while there is hope.

Father, I thank You that, as You have said, You have poured Your Spirit upon my seed and Your blessing upon my offspring. Father, I believe all my children will make Jesus the Lord of their lives because You said that if I believe on the Lord Jesus Christ, I would be saved and my house.

I believe Your Word is true. I will not worry or fear if it does not look like the things I have confessed are true now in my children's lives because I walk by faith, not by sight. I cast the care of my children's well-being—spirit, soul, and body—over on You, Father, for You care for me. I will not stagger at Your promises through unbelief, but will be strong in faith, giving You glory.

I am fully persuaded that what You have promised, You are able to perform and that You are doing it now!

Thank You, Father. Amen.

Now, expect results because it is impossible for God to lie!

Scripture References

Is. 54:13	Is. 44:3
Eph. 6:1-4	Acts 16:31
Col. 3:20,21	2 Cor. 5:7
Deut. 6:7	1 Pet. 5:7
Prov. 19:18	Rom. 4:20,21
Ps. 138:8	Heb. 6:18

Additional Scriptures

Is. 29:22-24	Jer. 31:16,17
43:5,6	46:27
49:25	Luke 1:17
	John 6:45

Prayer for Those in Authority

Father, we know from Your Word that by You kings reign and rulers decree justice. By You, princes and nobles, even all the judges and governors of the earth, rule.

We hold up before You now and give thanks in Jesus' name for those people in this nation in any position of authority over us: for our President, Vice-President, their cabinet and advisors; our federal, state, and local senators, congressmen, and judges; our governors and mayors; military leaders; other heads of government agencies and departments; policemen, school boards, and city councils.

According to Your Word, Father, we ask You in Jesus' name to remove and set up those officials whom You would.

We agree that divinely directed decisions are on their lips and that their mouths do not transgress in judgment. We agree that their hearts are in Your hand and that You turn them whichever way You will. You have made our leaders to be blessed and a blessing forever. Through Your mercy and steadfast love, they will never be moved.

Thank You for giving our leaders knowledge of Your way of judging, O God, and the Spirit

77

of Your righteousness to control all their actions. We declare that they judge and govern Your people with righteousness; the poor and afflicted with judgment and justice. They judge and defend the poor of the people, deliver the children of the needy, and crush the oppressor. Your right hand guides them to tremendous things.

We praise You, Lord, that our leaders winnow out all evil with their eyes. They winnow the wicked from among the good and bring the threshing wheel over them.

Loving-kindness, mercy, truth, and faithfulness preserve them. Their positions of authority are upheld by the people's loyalty.

We declare that because their ways please You, Lord, You have made even their enemies to be at peace with them. Thank You that the lying lips which speak insolently against them with pride and contempt are silenced. Thank You for hiding them in the secret of Your presence from the plots of men and for keeping them secretly in Your pavilion from the strife of tongues.

In Jesus' name, we declare that Americans do not, even in thought, curse their leaders, for the uncompromisingly righteous are in authority and the people rejoice. Because the fear of the believers will fall upon them, many people of the land submit themselves to the Word of God and become believers.

We declare that our government is established and made secure by righteousness. The stability of our nation will long continue because our leaders are men and women of discernment, understanding, and knowledge.

Our nation is elevated by uprightness and right standing with You, Father, because our leaders carefully listen to Your voice. We lend to many nations, but we do not borrow; we rule over many nations, but none rules over us.

In Jesus' name, we receive Your blessing for America because You, Father, are Lord. Amen.

Scripture References (AMP)

Deut. 15:5,6	Prov. 8:15,16
Ps. 31:18,20	14:34
33:2	16:7,10,12
72:1,2,4	20:8,26,28
Dan. 2:21	21:1
Acts 23:5	28:2
	29:2

Prayer for Finances

Father, I come to You in Jesus' name, giving You praise and glory for all You have provided for me in Christ Jesus. I set myself in agreement with Your Word, knowing that Your Word shall not return to You void, or useless, without producing any effect, but shall accomplish that which You please and purpose. It shall prosper in the thing for which it is sent.

You said in Your Word that You wish above all things that I prosper and be in health, even as my soul prospers. In the light of Your Word, I receive Your prosperity into my life. I believe that You are liberally supplying and filling (to the full) my every need according to Your riches in glory by Christ Jesus. I confess that Jesus has redeemed me from the curse of poverty. Poverty has no right to operate against me or my family, and I resist it in Jesus' name.

I am a cheerful giver. I give from my heart. Because of this, I believe that You, Father, are making all grace (every favor and earthly blessing) come to me in abundance. Because I am a giver and sow generously that blessings may come to others, I also reap generously with blessings.

I am always, in all circumstances, self-sufficient. I possess enough to require no aid or support and am furnished in abundance for every good work and charitable donation.

Father, I thank You for establishing prosperity in my life. It belongs to me. I walk in the blessings of the Lord. Everything I set my hands to prospers, in Jesus' name! Amen.

Scripture References (AMP)

Is. 55:11	3 John 2
Gal. 3:13	2 Cor. 9:6-8

Prayer for the Tithe

Father, in Jesus' name, I declare that I am not a God-robber by withholding my tithes and offerings. I am a tither, faithfully bringing all my tithes—the whole tenth of my income—into the storehouse that there may be food in Your house. Because I have, You have promised that the windows of heaven are opened to me, and the blessings being poured out are so abundant that there isn't room enough to receive them all.

I thank You that You have rebuked the devourer for my sake. He shall not destroy the fruits of my ground; neither shall my vine drop its fruit before the time in the field.

Thank You for it, in Jesus' name. Amen.

Scripture Reference
Mal. 3:8-10

Confession of Healing

Father, in Jesus' name, I praise You that Jesus Himself took (in order to carry away) my weaknesses and infirmities and bore away my diseases. According to Your Word, Jesus personally bore in His own body my sins. He offered Himself on the tree that I might cease to exist to sin and live to righteousness. By His wounds I have been healed.

In agreement with Mark 11:24, I pray and believe that I am healed *now*! My faith in Your Word is my proof that I am healed, regardless of what my body says.

I speak to my body right now: ''Body, I command you to get in line with the Word of God that says you have been healed. Now, you *act*, *look*, *sound*, *feel*, *taste*, and *smell* healed, in Jesus' name!''

I thank You, Father, that it is done now! I will not weaken in faith or consider my body. No unbelief or distrust will make me waver or doubtingly question concerning Your Word. I am strong, empowered by faith. In Jesus' name, I give praise and glory to You because I am fully satisfied that You are able and mighty to keep Your Word and do what You have promised. Amen.

Scripture References (AMP)

Is. 53:4,5   Mark 11:23,24
Matt. 8:17   Rom. 4:19-21
1 Pet. 2:24

Additional Scriptures
Concerning Healing

acne
  2 Sam. 14:25
arthritis
  Luke 13:11-16
barrenness
  Ps. 113:9
  Gal. 4:27
blessed offspring
  Is. 65:23
bones
  Ps. 34:20
  Prov. 3:8
broken heart
  Ps. 34:18
      147:3
death
  Ps. 33:19
ears
  Prov. 20:12
  Is. 35:5
eyes
  Is. 35:5
  Ps. 146:8
  Prov. 20:12

hemorrhaging
  Mark 5:29
lameness, dumbness
  Is. 35:6
miscarriage
  Ex. 23:26
oppression
  Ps. 9:9
sound mind
  2 Tim. 1:7
  1 Cor. 2:16
teeth
  Song of Sol. 6:6
  Gen. 49:12
weakness
  Is. 35:3
  Heb. 12:12
withered hand
  Mark 3:5

Life and Death
Situations

Isaiah 54:17 says that no weapon
formed against us shall prosper, and
every tongue that shall rise against us in
judgment we shall show to be wrong.
When you are faced with believing that
someone will live and receive his
healing when everyone around you is
telling you that it is impossible, the
following confession of faith will prove
to be invaluable to you.

When doctors say that nothing can
be done for someone, that he is sure to
die, you can stand on God's Word. You
can proclaim that the weapon (death)
that has been formed against him will
not prosper. You can speak that though
tongues have risen against him judging
that he will die, he will show those
judgments to be wrong and will live.

When we are praying for life and
death situations, we do what the
eleventh chapter of Mark describes

Jesus as doing. Verse 14 says Jesus spoke directly to the fig tree; He spoke the end result. So, *we* speak directly to the body of the person for whom we are praying and tell that body to live. On the basis of what Jesus told us to do (see vv. 23,24), we speak to death in Jesus' name and command it to leave. Then, we believe that we receive life for that person when we pray.

Once again, there is no distance in the spirit world. We don't have to be with the person to speak life to him; we *believe* it is done because of faith in God's Word. God is not a man that He should lie.

From that time on, we return God's Word to Him in prayer. His Word does not return to Him without producing any effect. It accomplishes what He purposes, and it prospers in the thing for which He sent it. Confess God's Word over the situation like this:

Father, in Jesus' name, I thank You that _____ shall not die, but shall live and declare Your works and recount Your illustrious acts. Though impossible with men, it is not with You, for all things are possible with You.

I will not weaken in faith and consider _____'s body; no unbelief or distrust will make me waver or doubtingly question concerning Your promise. I am strong and empowered by faith as I give praise and glory to You, for I am fully satisfied and assured that You are able and mighty to keep Your Word and to do what You have promised.

Your Word says that You will even deliver the one who is not innocent for whom I intercede through the cleanness of my hands. Whether or not the people for whom I pray are innocent, I believe that what I have spoken is done as a result of my intercession, because You are no respecter of persons. I thank You that it is done in Jesus' name. So be it!

As you pray this prayer from God's Word, you will see results. Jeremiah 1:12 says God is alert and active, watching over His Word to perform it. *Expect God to work in your behalf! He loves you!*

Scripture References (AMP)

Ps. 118:17	Rom. 4:19-21
Mark 10:27	Job 22:30

Prayer for the Unsaved

Father, I thank You that You sent Jesus to seek and to save that which was lost. Therefore, in the name of Jesus, I claim _____ into Your Kingdom.

Satan, according to Matthew 18:18, I bind you in _____'s life, and I render every spirit that has operated in his life to keep him from the will of God, helpless, blind, deaf, and dumb, in Jesus' name.

Father, I say that the god of this world can no longer blind _____'s mind, and that the light of the glorious Gospel of Christ is shining unto him, in Jesus' name! You have given unto _____ the spirit of wisdom and revelation in the knowledge of You. The eyes of his understanding are enlightened so that he knows the hope of Your calling.

I pray, Father, that You will send laborers into his pathway to tell him the Good News of the abundant life that Jesus has brought him. I say that he is not able to resist the intelligence, wisdom, and inspiration of the Spirit with which those laborers speak.

I thank You that _____ has recovered himself out of the snare of the

Devil and is no longer taken captive by him at his will. I believe, in Jesus' name, that _____ confesses with his mouth the Lord Jesus and believes in his heart that You have raised Jesus from the dead, and that _____ is saved.

I believe I receive these things right now as I pray. I will give You only praise from now on because these things are already done. You are watching over Your Word to perform it. I know that _____ is delivered because Your Word says You will deliver even the ones for whom I intercede who are not innocent through the cleanness of my hands.

Thank You for Your Word, Father, in Jesus' name. Amen.

Now, refuse to worry. Thank God for the salvation of the person for whom you were praying and walk by faith in God's ability, not by sight. *God will not fail you!*

Scripture References

Luke 19:10	Matt. 9:37,38
Eph. 1:17,18	Acts 6:10 AMP
John 10:10	Rom. 10:9,10
2 Tim. 2:26	Mark 11:24
Jer. 1:12	Job 22:30 AMP
2 Cor. 4:4	
5:7	

Additional Scriptures

Matt. 18:18   Luke 10:2

Additional Scriptures

Using *The Amplified Bible* will help you to better understand many of these Scripture references.

First of All . . .

Prov. 2:10-16,20-22   1 Tim. 2:1-4

(All in authority) All scriptures pertaining to kings and wisdom can be prayed for those in authority.

Temporal and Finances

Deut. 26	Mal. 3:8-12
Ps. 9:9	Luke 6:38
(Inflation)	2 Cor. 9:8-11
75:6,7	Phil. 4:19
(Promotion)	3 John 2

Employees and Employers

Eph. 6:5-9	Col. 3:22-25
	4:1

Singles

Gen. 2:18,24
24:40
Job 22:27,28
Ps. 23:1
34:9,10
37:4,5
Eccl. 4:9-12

Is. 34:16
54:4,5
58:14
Mark 11:25
John 10:4,5
1 Cor. 7:17
Heb. 13:5
James 1:5-7

Backsliders

Job 22:30
Is. 57:17,18
Matt. 9:37,38
Luke 10:2
John 6:45
10:28,29

Acts 6:10
Eph. 1:17,18
2 Tim. 2:26
1 John 5:16

Gluttony, Other
Excessiveness or Bad Habit

Ps. 141:3
Prov. 13:25
23:1-3
25:16
Mark 8:8
Luke 21:34

Acts 24:16
1 Cor. 6:12,13
9:27
2 Tim. 1:7
1 Pet. 4:2
1 John 5:21

References

The Amplified Bible, Old Testament. Published by Zondervan Publishing House, Grand Rapids, Michigan. Used by permission.

The Amplified Bible, New Testament. Published by The Lockman Foundation, La Habra, California. Used by permission.

The Bible: A New Translation. James Moffatt. Published by Harper & Row, Publishers, Inc., New York, New York. Used by permission.

The Living Bible. Published by Tyndale House Publishers, Wheaton, Illinois. Used by permission.

The New Testament: A New Translation by William Barclay. Published in Great Britain by William Collins Sons & Co. Ltd., and the U.S.A. by The Westminster Press. Used by permission.

The New Testament: An Expanded Translation. Kenneth S. Wuest. Published by William B. Eerdmans Publishing Company, Grand Rapids, Michigan. Used by permission.

The New Testament in Modern English. J. B. Phillips. Published by The Macmillan Company, New York, New York. Used by permission.

New Testament In Modern Speech. Richard Francis Weymouth. Published by Kregel Publications, Grand Rapids, Michigan. Used by permission.

The New Testament in the Translation of Monsignor Ronald Knox. Published by Andrews and McMeel, Inc., Kansas City, Kansas.

Weymouth's New Testament in Modern Speech. Richard Francis Weymouth. Published by Harper & Row, Publishers, Inc. and James Clarke and Company Ltd., New York, New York. Used by permission.

Dr. Ed Dufresne is a bold, compassionate minister with more than 26 years in the ministry.

Dr. Dufresne, who was reared a Catholic, had a startling call to the ministry. He was saved shortly afterwards and immediately began serving in the ministry of helps. He later pastored for a total of ten and a half years, and has traveled full-time for 20 years.

World Harvest School of Ministry, an outreach of Ed Dufresne Ministries, is a school that has been raised up to train believers in the operations of the Holy Spirit and in living a victorious life through the power of God's Word.

Other outreaches of Ed Dufresne Ministries are evangelistic tent crusades that reach out to the poor and needy in distributing food, clothing, and toys. In addition, weekly miracle crusades are held at the ministry headquarters in Temecula, California.

Dr. Dufresne has a mandate from heaven to take the healing power of Jesus to this generation as he travels throughout North America and around the world.

For more information about Ed Dufresne Ministries, to be placed on the mailing list, or if you have a prayer request, please contact the ministry at the address listed below:

Ed Dufresne Ministries
P.O. Box 186
Temecula, CA 92593